A Crabtree Branches Book

SERVING with Honor

NAVY

written by Bernard Conaghan

CRABTREE Publishing Company
www.crabtreebooks.com

School-to-Home Support for Caregivers and Teachers

This high-interest book is designed to motivate striving students with engaging topics while building fluency, vocabulary, and an interest in reading. Here are a few questions and activities to help the reader build upon his or her comprehension skills.

Before Reading:

- *What do I think this book is about?*
- *What do I know about this topic?*
- *What do I want to learn about this topic?*
- *Why am I reading this book?*

During Reading:

- *I wonder why...*
- *I'm curious to know...*
- *How is this like something I already know?*
- *What have I learned so far?*

After Reading:

- *What was the author trying to teach me?*
- *What are some details?*
- *How did the photographs and captions help me understand more?*
- *Read the book again and look for the vocabulary words.*
- *What questions do I still have?*

Extension Activities:

- *What was your favorite part of the book? Write a paragraph on it.*
- *Draw a picture of your favorite thing you learned from the book.*

Table of Contents

Mission

The United States Navy is one branch of the United States Armed Forces. It is responsible for **military operations** on water to keep the U.S. safe.

Values

Sailors are expected to live by values. The three core values are honor, courage, and commitment. They guide sailors' actions every day, whether on or off the job. The Sailor's **Creed** is an **oath** to these values.

Chief petty officer selectees recite the Sailor's Creed.

Navy
Medal of Honor

Fun Fact

The U.S. Navy and Marine Corps' Medal of Honor is the country's highest military award. It is given to sailors who show courage and bravery while risking their lives.

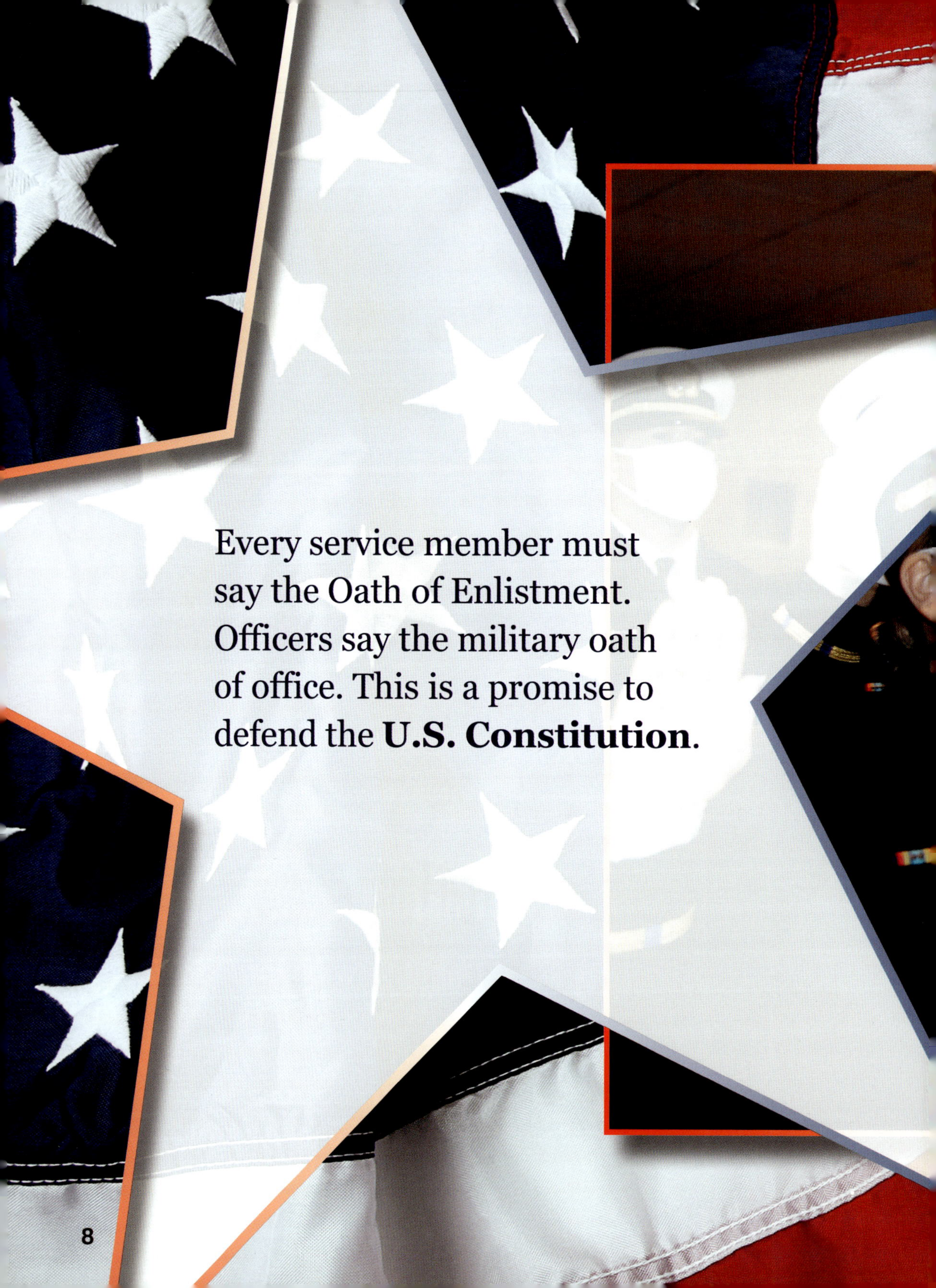

Every service member must say the Oath of Enlistment. Officers say the military oath of office. This is a promise to defend the **U.S. Constitution**.

Uniform

The Navy has strict rules for uniforms. Combat uniforms have **camouflage** and are easy to work in. Service uniforms have a button-up shirt. They can be worn every day. Dress or "mess" uniforms are the most formal. These are worn on special occasions.

Fun Fact

The Navy has darkened the traditional navy blue to almost black to try to stop fading.

Equipment and Vehicles

The Navy has different types of ships to carry out missions. An **aircraft carrier** is a moving airfield. Submarines go underwater for combat and research. Battleships, cruisers, and destroyers engage enemy forces on the water.

An F/A-18E Super Hornet

Nimitz-class aircraft carrier USS Harry S. Truman

Aircraft are also used by the Navy. Fighter planes destroy enemy aircraft in air-to-air combat. Airborne early warning planes use radar to find and follow targets. Transport planes have large cabins for passengers and cargo.

An E-2D Hawkeye, Carrier Airborne Early Warning Squadron

Fast-attack submarine USS Key West

Fun Fact

Navy SEALS carry gear that is durable and can adapt to any terrain, or type of land.

Having the right equipment is important. Night vision goggles help soldiers see in the dark. **Satellites** transmit information. Laser target locators help find targets.

Training

Sailors must be strong and ready for missions. **Recruit** training lasts about nine weeks. Sailors learn how to work as a team, discipline, and the Navy's core values. They also train in firefighting and water survival.

Advanced Individual Training (AIT) is next in "A" School. Sailors learn the skills needed for their military occupational specialty (MOS). AIT schools prepare sailors for specific jobs in the Navy.

Careers

The U.S. Navy has many different types of jobs for battle on the sea, on land, and in the air. Navy fighter pilots fly high-powered jets from decks of aircraft carriers. Intelligence specialists collect information about possible enemies.

Fun Fact

Many jobs in the Navy also prepare sailors for jobs as ***civilians****. Some technical training allows sailors to get a professional license from trade organizations.*

The U.S. Navy also has jobs that provide support to the troops. Culinary specialists prepare and serve the food. Cargo specialists make sure that equipment, supplies, and mail arrive wherever the troops are located.

Keeping equipment working is important. Electronics specialists repair electronics and safely disarm explosives. Mechanics keep ships and aircraft running.

Ways to Serve

There are two main ways to serve in the U.S. Navy. Active duty sailors live and work on a Navy base and on a ship full-time. Soldiers in the Navy Reserve serve part-time and can live anywhere in the United States.

Naval Reserve Officers Training Corps midshipmen practice patching a pipe with a soft patch during Sea Trials.

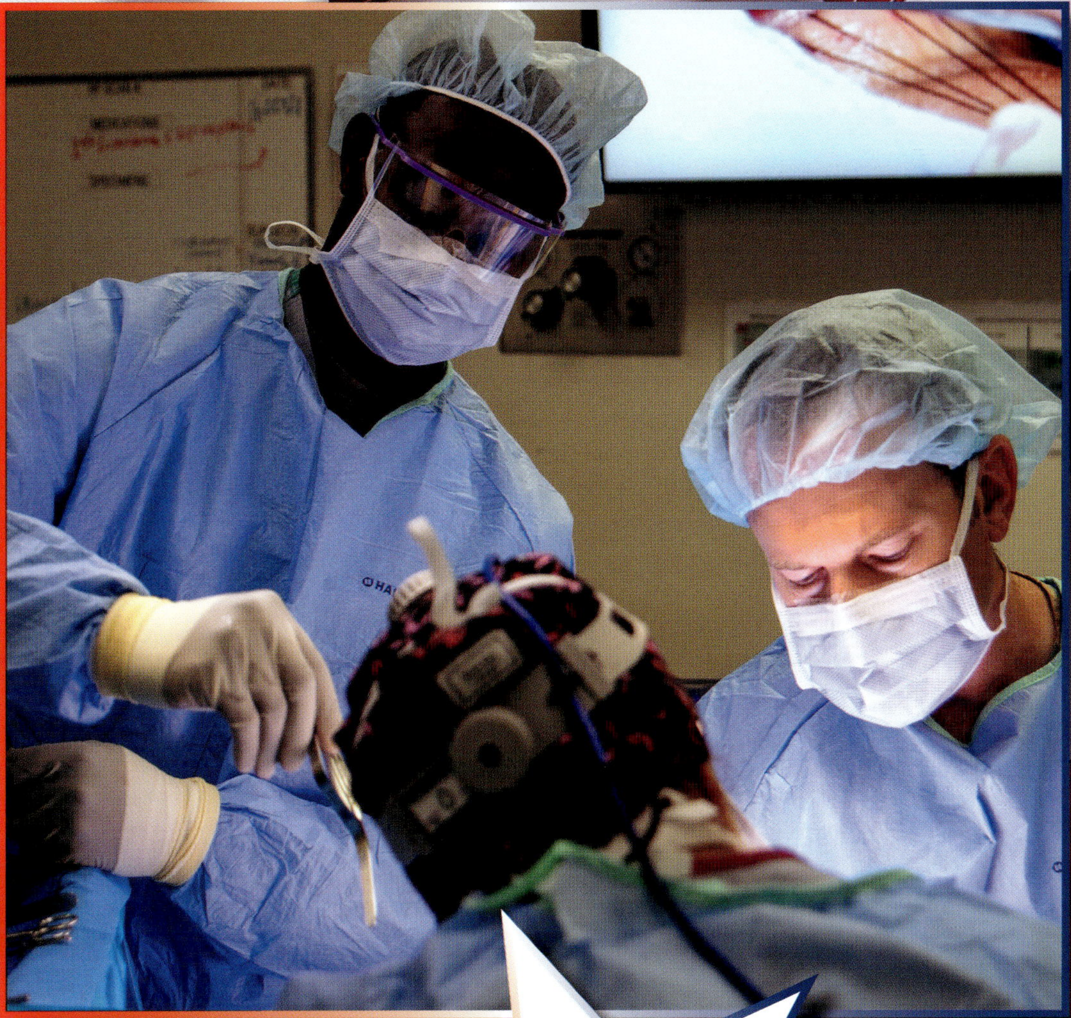

Fun Fact

Navy civilians are workers for the U.S. Navy but are not sailors. Jobs include cybersecurity, medicine, office work, and support for families on base.

The Navy has basic requirements to **enlist**. A person must be a U.S. citizen, between the ages of 17 and 39, and have a high school diploma. The Armed Services Vocational Aptitude Battery (ASVAB) tests a person's knowledge of reading, math, science, and thinking. A medical exam determines if a person is healthy and strong.

Showing Appreciation

Members of the Navy are on call every day of the year. They put their lives at risk to keep us safe. We celebrate them throughout the year. May is Military Appreciation month.

Thank You

HONORING ALL WHO SERVE

Veterans Day is a time to thank those who are serving. It is also for those who served in the past and are still living. Memorial Day is for remembering the men and women who lost their lives serving their country. Are you ready to serve in the U.S. Navy?

Glossary

aircraft carrier (**er**·kraft **ker**-ee-ər) A warship with a flight deck on which aircraft can be launched and landed

camouflage (**ka**·muh·flaazh) Disguising items to help someone blend in with their surroundings

civilian (suh·**vi**·lyn) Someone who is not in the armed forces or police

creed (kreed) A statement of beliefs

enlist (uhn·**list**) To join the armed forces

military operations (**mi**·luh·teh·ree aa·pr·**ay**·shnz) Armed actions in response to a situation

mission (**mi**·shn) An assignment

oath (owth) A promise

recruit (ruh·**kroot**) Enlisted in the armed forces

satellite (**sa**·tuh·lite) An item that is in Earth's orbit and communicates information

U.S. Constitution (kaan·stuh·**too**·shn) The rights and laws that are the basis of the government of the United States

Index

Websites

www.navy.mil
www.navy.com
www.militaryonesource.mil

About the Author

Bernard Conaghan lives in South Carolina with his German shepherd named Duke. His grandmother was the jeep driver for the Major General for the U.S. Marines during World War II. He is a coach on his son's football team. He always eats one scoop of peach ice cream after dinner.

CRABTREE Publishing Company

Written by: Bernard Conaghan
Designed by: Jen Bowers
Proofreader: Petrice Custance
Print Coordinator: Katherine Berti

Photographs: Cover and p.5 U.S. Navy photo/Seaman George Valceanu, U.S. flag ©2008 J. Helgason/Shutterstock; p.3 U.S. Navy photo/Lance Cpl. Danny Nateras; p.6 U.S. Navy photo/MCS 3rd Class Anderson W. Branch; p.7 U.S. Navy photo; p.9 U.S. Navy photo/MCS 2nd Class Derien C. Luce; p.10 ©2010 Keith McIntyre/Shutterstock; p.11 U.S. Navy photo/Candidate Officer Mark Abbott, U.S. Navy photo; p.12 U.S. Navy photo/MCSA Joshua Sapien, U.S. Navy photo/MCS 2nd Class Joshua M. Tolbert/; p.13 U.S. Navy photo/MCS 2nd Class Zachary Grooman, U.S. Navy photo/MCS 3rd Class Michael Singley; p.14 U.S. Navy photo/Lance Cpl. Grace Gerlach; p.15 U.S. Navy photo/Builder 3rd Class Alexa Trafton; p.17 U.S. Navy photo/Lance Cpl. Hope Straley; p.19 U.S. Navy photo/Naval Education and Training Command; p.20 U.S. Marine Corps photo/Sgt. Booker T. Thomas III; p.21 U.S. Navy photo/Equipment Operator 2nd Class Brandon Blevins; p.22 U.S. Navy photo/MCSA Michael Mensah; p.23 U.S. Navy photo/MCS 3rd Class Isaiah Williams; p.24 U.S. Navy photo/MCS 2nd Class Emilia C. Hilliard; p.25 U.S. Navy photo/MCS 3rd Class Luke Cunningham; p.27 ©2019 smolaw/Shutterstock; p.28-29 Black Creator 24/Shutterstock

Library and Archives Canada Cataloguing in Publication

Available at the Library and Archives Canada

Library of Congress Cataloging-in-Publication Data

Available at the Library of Congress

Crabtree Publishing Company

www.crabtreebooks.com 1-800-387-7650

Published in the United States
Crabtree Publishing
347 Fifth Avenue
Suite 1402-145
New York, NY, 10016

Published in Canada
Crabtree Publishing
616 Welland Ave.
St. Catharines, ON
L2M 5V6

Printed in the U.S.A./072022/CG20220201